CW00545987

Flower Recipes and Rituals

Titania's Crystal Heart

Flower Recipes and Rituals

Titania Hardie

Photography by
Emma Peios

CONNECTIONS
BOOK PUBLISHING

A CONNECTIONS EDITION

This edition published in Great Britain in 2004 by
Connections Book Publishing Limited
St Chad's House, 148 King's Cross Road
London WC1X 9DH
www.connections-publishing.com

British Library Cataloguing-in-Publication data available on request.

ISBN 1-85906-157-5

10 9 8 7 6 5 4 3 2 1

Phototypeset in Ocean Sans using QuarkXPress on Apple Macintosh
Origination by Pixel Tech, Singapore
Printed and bound by Hung Hing Offset Printing Co. Ltd, China

Contents

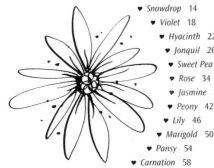

Valentine hearts... and flowers

In ancient Rome, the month of February was named for Juno Februata, the patroness of passion or the 'fever of love'. Aptly, the pagan festival of *Lupercalia* began on 15 February. This was a joyful fertility rite that honoured Lupercus, a rustic fertility god, and included feasting, dancing and some socially sanctioned sexual behaviour that went way beyond flirting! The date coincided with the moment when love birds appeared to pair off for the coming spring. On the very eve of this festival, 14 February, every young man would draw the name of one girl out of an olive jar, and they would be partners in merriment for the whole of the festival period.

st valentine

St Valentine appears to have entered the story by way of association. He was a Roman priest of the third century, who was imprisoned after he outraged Emperor Claudius II by boldly marrying young couples against his wishes – the emperor believed that married men were unwilling soldiers! Valentine is said to have fallen deeply in love with the beautiful daughter of his gaoler, whose blindness he miraculously cured through his love and faith. When he was taken away to be executed on the eve of Lupercalia, the ill-fated lover left his sweetheart a poignant message (some say on the wall of his cell) that was signed 'From your Valentine'. In 498, Pope Galasius tried to quash the pagan practice of celebrating St Valentine's Day on his anniversary, but custom victoriously fused the strands of love and courtship, and the saint's romantic words have echoed through almost two millennia, with every greeting on 14 February still signed with his phrase.

the birds and the bees

Many Valentine rituals are derived from the birds. One tradition tells that if the first bird a woman sees on St Valentine's Day is a robin, she'll marry a sailor, while if she sees a sparrow first, her partner will be poor. If you are wishing for a good provider, emulate the girl who spies a goldfinch – she will marry into prosperity! If you see a dove or pigeon, your partner will always be true; and if you see a bee on the day – which is early in the season – your life will be as sweet as honey, and you will meet your true sweetheart. But another tradition may stem from Valentine curing his beloved's blindness: that you will marry the first person of the opposite sex who you see on this day! In days gone by, some girls blindfolded themselves or held their eyes tightly shut all day, to avoid seeing the wrong man!

valentine hearts ... and flowers

an ancient valentine's ritual

This ritual dates to the Middle Ages. It was to ensure you 'saw' the right partner for love. At midnight, as Valentine's Day began, brave girls would circle the churchyard twelve times, scattering seeds of hemp between the graves, saying: *'I sow hemp seed; Hemp now I sow; Come now my love: Follow and mow.'* If the magic was strong, the girls would be able to see the ghostly forms of their future husbands gathering the seed behind them. Not for the faint-hearted! If this was too much, you could go to bed on Valentine's Eve with your shoes placed in a 'T' shape, saying: *'I form my shoes as a letter T; With hopes that my true love I'll see; In his apparel, his array; As he is now and every day.'* A dream would then reveal the face of your beloved. Sweet dreams!

the first valentine's card ...

One of the first people to send a 'valentine' was Charles, Duc d'Orléans, who, in 1415, while imprisoned in the Tower of London, sent rhyming poems and love letters to his wife. The British Library holds what is thought to be the oldest existing valentine – a fifteenth-century card sent by Marjorie Paston to her husband John, depicting a knight and a lady with Cupid's arrow piercing the armoured knight's heart. Cupid, the son of Venus, was not always a friend to lovers. His childish pranks were sometimes poorly aimed darts of love sent to someone whose feelings might never be returned. Venus herself, whose emblem was the rose, was less callous in her feelings for mortals, and so the rose became the goodwill token for true love, and the best message for a Valentine.

In Europe, in the seventeenth century, lovers made valentines by copying verses of poetry, perhaps with drawings or paintings. In the eighteenth century in England, it was customary to draw lots for a Valentine partner; in ancient Rome, if a gentleman liked a lady, the custom was to give her first a pair of gloves, and then a kiss! Around 1800, the first commercially made valentines appeared; at this time they tended to be very basic. In the more sentimental Victorian era, valentines were wrought with lace, silk and imitation jewels; and from the 1830s, Esther Howland in Worcester, Massachusetts, used fine imported paper and fabric to create the first home-grown American valentines for sale in the mass market. The tradition of giving chocolates and honeyed sweets possibly recalls the superstition of finding a bee on St Valentine's Day, which promised that you would find your sweetheart.

... and flowers

Scented blooms were asked to carry a lover's message because of propriety: in the eighteenth and nineteenth centuries, decorum prevented a courting couple spending time alone together, or even corresponding, until they were actually engaged. How were they ever to reach that stage if they couldn't talk privately? Gardens were acceptable places for couples to walk in, and flowers became an elaborate language – ambassadors of human feelings and hopes. They also captured the magic and fairy lore of centuries, bearing scented spirits that might just sway a heart that was undecided! So it seems entirely appropriate to celebrate St Valentine's Day with the souls of flowers, to remind ourselves of the magical powers that can be spoken year-long by their voices. They may keep your heart and your spirits blooming, and attract enchantment and love throughout the year.

The Flowers

When we gather a bouquet or send flowers to a loved one, we create a harmony with nature, and this bestows a sense of well-being and peace. When we understand the magical connections of flowers and plants, we drink up their ancient mystery and power, gathered from the bosom of the earth itself. Flowers are a gift of the earth's spirit – her messengers of wisdom, providing a store cupboard to healers and wise-women the world over. In the pages that follow, you will learn something of their blessings to us all – and absorb some gentle sorcery that makes them the soul mates of all lovers, and those beloved. Display the flower-of-the-month cards in the lovely glass paperweight, to make the most of each bloom at its peak (you can even make your own cards using pictures of your favourite flowers). If you're in Australia, simply shuffle the order of the flowers to suit the season. Each card includes a 'wish' spell to help you use the essence of the flowers, to bring passion and magic to your day.

Snowdrop *hope*

It is usually assented in the Northern Hemisphere that the snowdrop is the first bulb (if not flower) to bloom in the year. Seen by some as an omen of winter descending on a relationship, it has happier associations as the flower that protected Odysseus from Circe's enchantment, keeping him faithful to his homeland. For centuries, this delicate, but hardy, little flower has been connected with purity and harmony in the grey landscape, a harbinger of joy and the returning Maiden of Spring. It is the flower of hope, tenacity and loyalty, confidently forecasting a revival in matters of the heart. If your beloved has broken your heart, a snowdrop blooming nearby guarantees that love will grow again. Also known as the 'fair maid of winter', the flower's language tells us: 'I make a new bid for your deepest affections'. Plant snowdrops in the garden, and angels will come near.

the *Snowdrop* oracle

*Snowdrops were traditionally thought of as fairy spirits.
Thus, they are perfect omens of the future, especially as
they bloom with the new year. When snowdrops appear,
try this ritual.*

Place a single snowdrop in a glass vase beside your bed.
Gaze at its petals and remain silent until you sleep. Ask to
dream of your future love.

♥ If you dream of picking snowdrops, you will have a very
happy year, and a wonderful surprise in love.

♥ If you dream of smelling a snowdrop, you must grab
hold of an opportunity that is already before you.

♥ To dream of a basket of snowdrops means a wedding
approaches; a posy of snowdrops indicates a birth.

♥ If you see snowdrops in a circlet, this means you will
have a new love.

♥ Dreaming of the flowers growing under a tree says your
spirit is blessed, and your love will blossom.

flowers in the kitchen: *Snowdrop* biscuits

These little flowers have never been used in food, as far as I know, but the cookies take their name from the shape, and have a fairy spirit about them!

gather together

whites of 3 large eggs; ¼ teaspoon cream of tartar; 1 teaspoon vanilla essence; 1 teaspoon white vinegar; 175 g (6 oz) caster sugar; 125 g (4 oz) chocolate chips

♥ Beat the egg whites until stiff. Add the cream of tartar, vanilla essence and white vinegar, then gradually add the caster sugar, beating between additions. Finally, fold in the chocolate chips, and drop teaspoons of the mixture onto a grease-proof baking sheet. Bake in a very hot oven at 240°C/475°F/Gas Mark 9 for 20 minutes, then turn off the oven and leave the biscuits inside to cool for a further 20 minutes. The insides should be slightly gooey. Serve with a caffe latte, and strew snowdrops on the plate of biscuits.

flowers in the shower: *Snowdrop* shampoo

*Present research verifies an old claim that snowdrops can
be made into a medicine which improves memory; perhaps
using this shampoo will keep someone you love at the front
of your mind? It will also keep your spirit serene and strong.*

gather together

a few snowdrop heads (try to use a fragrant variety);
30 ml (1 fl oz) pure alcohol; 100 ml (3½ fl oz) baby shampoo

♥ Steep the snowdrop heads in the pure alcohol (available
from pharmacies and herbal suppliers). Leave for 24 hours,
before adding the ingredients to the baby shampoo. Agitate
the mixture daily for three days, then shampoo your hair.
As you massage it in, think of someone you'd like to receive
a call from. Can you reach the phone from your shower?
♥ Also, try *Snowdrop Essence*, which is available from
Findhorn Flower Essences (*see page 62*). It is designed to
help combat those wintry feelings, or to cure a grey mood.

Violet ✳ modesty and quiet beauty

The violet's delicate appearance belies many romantic
secrets! The scent unites innocence with sensuality and
mystery, which perhaps accounts for its magic. Beloved
of Napoleon (nicknamed 'Corporal Violette' because
of his enchantment with the flower), Charles II,
and the last Empress of China, the tiny bloom
has a heady scent that you can only breathe for
a moment: after a few seconds, your olfactory
bulb must close off and rest! Used in sweets and
confections for centuries, violets also laced wine for
Roman ladies who hoped to mask their drinking with
the lovely scent! Violet wine may even remedy a hangover
itself. The heart-shaped leaves have many properties, and
made into a tea or a potion they ease headaches and
sore throats. But their potency for the heart made their
reputation. Few love-philtres or potpourri recipes omit
these flowers.

the *Violet* pharmacy

Make a romance-inducing potion for your skin with this
ancient British recipe, adapted from a tenth-century herbal.

gather together

3 tablespoons fresh violet flowers (*not* African violets, but
Viola odorata – sweet violets); 90 ml (3¼ fl oz) goat's milk

♥ Steep the flowers in the goat's milk for 2 hours at room
temperature. Use a mortar and pestle to make a paste, then
seal and refrigerate for 24 hours. Ensuring that your face is
cleansed, apply some of the paste as a mask and leave for
about 20 minutes, then tissue off.

♥ For a weaker solution to use as a light cleanser, process
the same amount of violets in 200 ml (7 fl oz) goat's milk,
and keep in the refrigerator: it will last for a week to ten days.

♥ Use a few violets steeped in spring water for three days
as a perfect accompanying skin tonic.

elixir of *Violets*

To emulate those sensuous Roman courtesans, brew this love-wine to leave your breath fresh enough to invite close contact with someone special. It may also boost fertility!

gather together

1 cup fresh violets (or 2 tablespoons dried violet leaves and flowers); 300 ml (½ pint) water; 50 g (2 oz) sugar

♥ Brew the flowers in the water and sugar. Bring to the boil over a low heat and simmer for 10 minutes. Then cool the solution, pour into a bottle, and cork. Allow this to develop for several days, then add a splash, like a cordial, to very dry white wine. Wow! Flirting material!

♥ To help ease a hangover, make a circlet of violets to place around the temples.

♥ And to banish gremlins, bad witches and ill spirits, make a slightly larger circlet to wear around your neck.

valentine profiteroles with *Violet* cream sauce

If you're good with pastry, whistle up some choux profiterole cases yourself; if you want to use shop-bought ones, that's fine too. The divine chocolate sauce is a must-have – in any form – for a Valentine pudding if you want to get very, very amorous with your beloved!

gather together

12 luxury violet chocolates (with crystallized flowers on top); 100 g (3½ oz) good-quality dark chocolate; 6 profiterole cases; 6 tablespoons whipped cream

♥ Remove the crystallized flowers from the chocolates. Put all the chocolate into a bain-marie and melt, over a low heat, to pouring consistency (add a little butter if it needs thinning). Fill the profiterole cases with whipped cream and the chocolate mixture, and pour extra (or ice cream) over the arranged profiteroles. Scatter the crystallized flowers on the top: watch the love-temperature rise!

Hyacinth *enchanted devotion*

Beloved above all flowers by the Marquise de Pompadour, mistress of Louis XV, in the eighteenth century, beautiful Dutch hyacinths are the cultivars of *Hyacinthus orientalis*, a native of Turkey and Iran. They are also related to the English wild hyacinth, or bluebell. These ancestors of the modern hyacinth were prized for their delicious scent and now, as before, they rain heavenly odours upon us in the early spring. The bloom is one of special enchantment, springing, according to legend, from the blood shed after a jealous quarrel between Apollo and Zephyr, which ended in the death of the beautiful Hyacinthus. To this day, it is wise to protect the hyacinths in your garden from the fierce west winds of the early spring, yet when given in a bouquet they allegedly bring laughter into the house!

hyacinth in the linen cupboard

Fresh hyacinth flowers are toxic, so handle them carefully and keep them away from your pets. However, treated properly, the flowers can be dried to form the focus of a superb potpourri that is lucky for love. It will reward the effort involved.

gather together

2 cups hyacinth petals (blend two colours – either pink or blue with white); ½ cup mixed fresh herbal leaves; 1 tablespoon dried orris root (available from a florist or pharmacy); a few drops hyacinth essential oil

♥ Mix together all the ingredients and enclose in an airtight jar. Keep the jar in a dark, warm place for six weeks, shaking it once each week. Transfer the potpourri to a bowl beside your bed, or use it to fragrance bedlinen. It will protect you from bad dreams and also boost your self-esteem.

wild *Hyacinths* in the bathroom

For extra resilience, or if someone else's grumpy mood is getting you down, make your own wild-hyacinth (also known as bluebell) toiletries. They will bring your laughter back, and also help you attract happiness in love.

♥ Get hold of the raw ingredients needed for making your own soap (*for suppliers, see pages 62–3*), and make some with a wild-hyacinth scent.

♥ For use in the bath: add 6 drops hyacinth essential oil (it's expensive but will last well; buy a tiny bottle) to 2 tablespoons full-cream milk, and disperse in running water. Sink low and empty your mind.

♥ For a satiny spring body, mash some soft, ripe fruit (peaches or apricots, perhaps) and add 1 tablespoon yoghurt and 4 drops hyacinth essential oil. Smooth over your body after bathing; rinse clean at once. Your love will cut through thorns to find you!

to bring fairy blessings into the home

Emulate the famous beauty, the Marquise de Pompadour, who forced hyacinths to grow early in the royal palaces of France, by growing them under glass (yes, we still follow her fashion at Christmas time!). This invites passionate love into your life, and will affect everyone else, too.

♥ According to tradition, magic works with the number three, so plant three bulbs in a deep dish or china bowl, and cover with a cloth or place in a sunny window. If you choose blue flowers, you're saying: 'I shall devote my love to you.' White flowers carry the message: 'I admire you beyond everyone.' Growing the blooms indoors will offset stress and grief, and create a calm and forgiving atmosphere. Send one bloom to your love, if you need forgiveness! Beside your bed, the flower will give you deep and beautiful dreams, and attract confessions of love from your amour!

Jonquil *fragrant joy*

From the genus *Narcissus*, these fragrant blossoms have a murky past, as they're associated with the flowers that bloomed in memory of Narcissus, the youth who fell in love with his own reflection and pined away. However, other myths are more generous, in the spirit of the exotic fragrance and sweetness of the jonquil; they have been beloved in England and Holland since the sixteenth century.

Bringing yellow fragrant blooms indoors brings good luck, while white flowers ensure good marriage prospects – but always pick a bunch rather than a single stem. As with daffodils, avoid trampling on jonquils in the grass, to spare a fairy spirit and find luck and thanks. Treat the blooms as friends; give them in posies to spread good fortune and joy, and to reflect one of their common names, which is 'cheerflower'.

the *Jonquil* pharmacy

The essential oil distilled from the narcissus is, of course, the fragrant variety – the famous Narcissus poeticus *– which has many properties in common with* Narcissus jonquilla. *Use the essential oil to attract not the destructive self-love fatal to Narcissus, but a wonderful state of relaxation and tranquillity. The fragrance inspires hypnotic stillness and creativity.*

♥ Add 3 drops narcissus essential oil to 1 teaspoon almond oil, and diffuse in an oil burner just before bedtime. Your dreams will be visionary and truthful.

♥ If you feel hopeless or disillusioned, add to your bath 6 drops of narcissus oil in 30 ml (1 fl oz) milk. Your tensions will melt away.

♥ For a massage that quashes nerves and promotes sensuality, blend 10 drops narcissus oil with 30 ml baby oil. Bliss!

Jonquil : your messenger of love

What flower could do more to sway a lover when you have quarrelled, or had a misunderstanding? To write subtle, magical love notes as a subtext to more obvious words of emotion, try using a fountain pen and scented ink to move your beloved to deepest empathy. Keep your words simple, and let the flower notes speak eloquently on your behalf.

♥ Use mauve or light-blue ink, and add to it 3 drops jonquil fragrance or narcissus essential oil. Use scented stationery, too – soak a cotton-wool pad with the oil and enclose it with the writing paper for at least 48 hours. When you've written your love note and put it in the envelope, add two jonquil petals and seal. Now, wait for some magic to happen. Do not allow yourself to pine any longer!

benign *Jonquil* sorcery

This old spell works when you want someone to fall deeply in love with you, but it must be someone who is free! Never use it on anyone whose heart is already given.

♥ In a flower-press, preserve **three** jonquils (the number is important), coloured **yellow** unless the spell concerns a love who has not contacted you for a while – in which case, use **white blooms**. Press the flowers on pretty, absorbent paper, and dust a little salt on the petals, both to conserve colour and scent, and to add magic (salt is precious in magic). Tighten the screws and place in a dark area. After ten days, put the flowers in a frame, and position a mirror nearby. On a new moon, say: '*My love, echo my love.*' If true feeling does exist between you, you will soon have proof of it.

Sweet Pea tender passion

This delicious scented bloom, originally from Sicily, is descended from the pea flower; it is a gift from the goddess to lift fatigued spirits at the day's end. It restores innocence after a harsh truth, and nerves after a shock. One of the truest enchanter's flowers, its magic has been released on the late-spring breezes to whisper magical charms and words of love to someone who is away from you. The flowers are synonymous with passion and tenderness combined, and can be given, or used in spells, to ask forgiveness of a friend or a love. When used in perfume or potpourri, the fragrance is helpful for recovery from an upset or illness, and some say it provides protection from ghosts and bad spirits. Red flowers are a symbol of true, though innocent, love; white sweet peas say: 'You are sweet, but I love another.'

oracle of the *Sweet Pea*

♥ These flowers can tell your fortune. Grow some in your garden, or in a pot or window box. Pluck the first flowers of the season as they open (often late in May) and tie them into a little bunch bound with pink ribbon or a strand of your hair. Sit outside with these flowers, and let nature tell you …

… If the first creature you see is a **snail**, you must be patient, for something special is unfolding; if it is a **ladybird**, very good fortune is prophesied; if a **bee**, travel is looming, and if the bee also lands on you, money is signified; if a **beetle**, slow down at work or illness may follow; if a **spider**, show it kindness, and a gift of jewels will come to you; and if it is a **grasshopper**, you will hear excellent news.

Sweet Pea soup for lovers

Sweet peas are unsuitable for this, so it's made from English peas, which, in their shells, are called 'sweet peas'. This minted pea soup is, according to tradition, lucky for lovers.

gather together

a little olive oil; 1 medium onion; 1 iceberg lettuce, shredded; 500 g (1 lb) fresh peas, shelled; 750 ml (1¼ pints) chicken or vegetable stock; 1 cup fresh mint leaves; sugar and salt to taste; 175 ml (6 fl oz) cream; 6 sweet-pea flowers

♥ Heat the oil in a pan and sauté the onion until translucent. Add the lettuce and peas, and cook until tender (about 8 minutes). Add the stock, simmer for 15 minutes, then remove from the heat. Add the mint and process in a blender. Reheat the soup, then season with sugar and salt. Serve hot or cold with a drizzle of cream. Garnish with a sweet-pea flower (on the side, for decoration only!). Toast 'the divine lady' for luck, as you begin eating.

three-flower potpourri for single ladies

If you're not lucky in love, this recipe will attract grace from Venus – these flowers honour her, and lend their enchanting fragrance to magically draw a love!

gather together

2 cups each **fragrant** sweet-pea petals, rose petals and lavender buds and leaves; 500 g (1 lb) coarse sea salt and fine salt (half and half)

♥ Place a layer of the petals (they need only be partly dried) in a large crock, sprinkle some salt over the top, and continue layering like this. Stand the crock, uncovered, in a dry, well-ventilated position for ten days. Then, transfer the blend to an airtight container (if it forms a cake, crumble it up) and steep for six weeks in a dark place. Put the potpourri into a bowl with a lid, and place it in your lounge area. For one month, each evening after 6 pm, light a candle and remove the lid of the potpourri. Things will happen!

Rose romantic seduction

The oldest flower, surely, to be associated with love, this extraordinary bloom was, according to legend, born with Venus, goddess of love, and is also beloved of Bacchus and Cupid. The rose was a favourite of the Empress Josephine, and her obsession was nothing new: Cleopatra plunged Antony knee-deep into rose petals to seduce him; harem brides are bathed in rosewater; and Romans sprinkled the petals of damask roses (the ancestor of our modern-day confetti) on wedding sheets. For a romantic dinner on any night – but especially in summer, when truly scented flowers emerge and might be plucked from your garden or terrace – add rose petals (pinch the white base off first) to whipped creams, ices, pastries and meringues. Stretch a trail of petals from the table to the bedroom – Cleopatra and Josephine knew a thing or two!

to recreate valentine's day at midsummer ...

*I have chosen two divinely romantic, but simple, recipes
to celebrate love in summer; you can also make these in
February, but you'll need to seek out scented, organic roses.*

Rose petal sorbet
gather together

150 ml (¼ pint) water; 150 g (5 oz) sugar; petals from 6
fragrant, pink roses; 2 teaspoons lemon juice; 1 teaspoon
glycerine; 250 ml (8 fl oz) full-cream milk

♥ Boil the water in a saucepan, add the sugar and dissolve.
Add the petals and simmer for 2 minutes, then remove from
the heat. Cool overnight, ensuring the petals are submerged.
Then strain the liquid, discarding the petals, and add the
lemon juice, glycerine and milk. Stir well, then churn in
an ice-cream maker for 15 minutes. Freeze until required.
Serve with whipped cream and petals for decoration. It
makes a superb accompaniment to the cake that follows ...

Rose valentine's cake
gather together

3 medium eggs; 115 g (4 oz) caster sugar; 75 g (3 oz) ground almonds; 50 g (2 oz) ground walnuts; 40 g (1½ oz) fresh white breadcrumbs; 2 teaspoons rosewater; icing sugar and rose petals to garnish

♥ Grease and flour a 20-cm (8-inch) heart-shaped cake tin. Beat together the eggs and sugar until light and pale. Fold in the nuts and breadcrumbs with a metal spoon; add the rosewater and fold carefully, keeping light and aerated. Spoon the mixture into the prepared tin and bake at 180°C, 350°F/Gas Mark 4 for 25–30 minutes. The cake is ready when it shrinks from the sides of the tin. Garnish with icing sugar and rose petals. Serve with whipped cream strewn with rose petals if desired, or with rose-petal sorbet and cream.

'By thy scent, my soul is ravished', says the Persian poet, Sadi. So will you!

Roses to rescue love

Roses can prophesy all regarding a love affair. Try the following:

♥ Add red, or deep pink, rose petals to your bath to conjure a lover, or to meet someone new.

♥ Wash your hands with rose-scented soap through the day, so the opposite sex will find you alluring.

♥ To make a love potion extra potent, wash with rosewater before you start work.

♥ Place rose petals in a small velvet bag and pin it to your underwear. This will bring you luck in love.

♥ Wear a fresh rose in your hair to draw love to you.

♥ Avoid harming a rose or trampling on its petals, for this takes your love for granted.

♥ Place rose petals carefully into a muslin bag and use these to shower a couple at their wedding. They will thrive, and you will be lucky in love, too.

Jasmine *sensual elegance*

This climbing shrub has an intense, honey-sweet perfume that has a narcotic effect. Legend has it that a wedding will occur if you bring a stem of the scented flowers into the house; and if you place a branching bough of partially opened flowers in the boudoir, erotic dreams will fill your night. Once the flowers open fully, you will gain erotic mastery over your beloved. Flowering – with luck – from June to early September, the plant is valued both for its beauty and scent, and should be grown around courtyards and windows for its romantic nocturnal fragrance. In the East, jasmine is offered at temples; in the West, it has been a key ingredient in love-philtres! The perfume suggests mystery, and invites adventure. A sprig worn in the hair can take flirtation to new heights, and the essential oil helps to develop your sensuality.

a Jasmine love potion

A powerful call upon the goddess of love (apples are her favourite fruit), this is a sensual summer treat that breaks down inhibitions!

gather together

1 teaspoon fresh jasmine flowers; 1 teaspoon fresh mint leaves, chopped; 500 ml (17 fl oz) apple juice; a few ice cubes; 2 tablespoons sugar; 1 green apple, peeled, cored and sliced; 2 jasmine flowers, for decoration; 250 ml (8 fl oz) champagne, optional

♥ Sprinkle the jasmine flowers and mint leaves into about half the apple juice, add the ice, and chill in the refrigerator for 2–3 hours. Wet the rim of two champagne glasses and coat with the sugar. Pour in the juice and add a garnish of sliced apples and one jasmine flower to each glass. Top up with a little champagne, if desired. Words won't be necessary!

Jasmine weekend break: an invitation

Plan a romantic weekend away and send your lover an invitation for a 'weekend of mystery', written in jasmine-scented ink (add 3 drops jasmine essential oil or fragrance to a pot of ink). Be enigmatic about the itinerary. Try to find a romantic hideaway; but the real magic will come if you use a jasmine-scented pillow to cradle your love's head …

gather together

1 cup jasmine flowers; 4 cups rose petals; 3 cups any othe
scented leaves, including marjoram; 2 drops each jasmine
rose and neroli essential oils

♥ Mix together all the flowers, petals and leaves, and add
the essential oils (all expensive, but irreplaceable!). Put thi
potpourri into a lace pouch (to tuck inside the pillow case
when the time comes), and pack it in your suitcase … along
with a blindfold! Produce these props at the appropriate
moment, and use them according to your own imagination

the floral body

Jasmine is an excellent flower to use to create an erotic body powder – more personal than commercial talc!

Into a small cardboard box with a lid (an old writing-paper box works well) sprinkle a layer of cornstarch or arrowroot, then add a layer of fresh jasmine flowers. Top with another layer of cornstarch or arrowroot, and repeat the process until you have at least three layers of flowers, then fit the lid. Leave to infuse for a few days, then take out any wilted flowers and replace with another layer of fresh ones. Leave for a few weeks so the scent can deepen. You'll soon have a delicate, fragrant powder that is personal to you. Dust it over your body and your bedlinen to encourage romance; and dust a little in your lingerie drawer to lift your spirits, and make you brave about love!

Peony ancient blessings

'How radiant is your beauty,' says this majestic blossom.
Named for Paeon, god of healing, this flower was the
favourite of the beautiful concubine Yang Kuei-fei, and
has been in the Imperial Gardens of Peking since
the fourth century. Symbolic, in the Oriental
world, of prosperity, luxury and happiness, you
should always grow a peony if you wish for
material peace. Even a painting of the flower will
help to bring abundance! This exquisite flower –
like an exotic rose – was sacred to the sun god Apollo,
and the sign Leo. It contains blessings enough, some
say, to assure transcendence for humanity. Though it has
a subtle scent that invites close encounter, smell a peony
when you are weary or despondent; if you need forgiveness
from a woman, this is your kindest ambassador.

white *Peony* for luck

Once used as an antidote to witchcraft, white peonies
have a beautiful, sweet scent – though still they are shy,
and ask you to get close! White peonies are said to be an
embodiment of moonbeams: they were credited with
protecting harvests and, in the home, averting destruction
from storms.

♥ Place a peony (either growing or cut) where it will catch
the moonlight; it will bring you visionary dreams of wild
inspiration and advice from the gods.

♥ If you have one that blooms at midsummer, first enjoy it
growing, then preserve the flower in a potpourri or flower
press. According to Claudius Aelianus, a first-century Roman
writer, the solstice peony yields: 'in the night-time a certain
fairy, as it were, sparkling brightness and white light.'

♥ If you grow a peony, it will reward you; but they are
slightly toxic, so cannot be eaten.

red and pink *Peonies*

♥ Red and pink peony petals will add a delicate fragrance to a potpourri and, crucially, add beauty and colour. Treat them with orris root and mix with other petals such as rose, and lemon verbena leaves, following the method given for 'hyacinths in the linen cupboard' (*see page 23*).

♥ In floral arrangements, peonies will help you to prosper; cut stems in your home ward off negativity and bad thoughts, as well as ill luck and lethargy. Pink and red blooms are especially lucky for matters of the heart, and if a sweetheart gives you a bunch, you will both enjoy good fortune with money as well as in love.

♥ If you are nervous, or anxiously facing a task, a peony in the lapel will guard your body and your spirit.

♥ Grow pink peonies with borage or sweet cicely, to bring fairies into your garden!

Peony for prosperity

♥ Acquire some silk of a peony hue (generally a strong pink, but you must appease yourself as to the colour!); it must be long enough to tie around your head or hair. Impregnate some tissue paper with a few drops of peony perfume oil (this is difficult to find; try the list of suppliers on pages 62–3). On a full moon, wrap the silk in the tissue paper. Now, leave them, undisturbed, for a fortnight, while the scent enters the fabric. Two weeks later, on the night of the new moon, wrap the fabric around your hair or whole head, and ask Diana of the Moon to honour you with some luxury or added prosperity. Sit quietly for one hour, then place the silk back in its tissue. The following morning, ask Apollo the Sun to favour your whole day, and wear the scarf once more. Good luck will find you!

Lily

womanly beauty and truth

According to folklore, the lily is the emblem of innocence
and purity, and was believed to grow of its own volition
on the graves of anyone unjustly accused or condemned.
One of the flowers most beloved of fairy folk, and
identified, too, with the Madonna, its scent offers
enigmatic insights and deepest intuitions. It is a
powerful messenger of love and passion: the tiger
lily speaks of undying devotion and longing; the
more modest white lily says: 'I kiss your fingertips.'
In magic, the lily is used to induce narcotic sleep,
and to wrap lovers in an embrace of sensuality, despite
its message of purity! Sleeping with a lily beside your bed
will bring dreams that tell you of anyone who gossips
about you or spreads rumour; and if you offer that person
a lily, you will remedy all injury in the dream world itself.

grow a magical Madonna *Lily*

*Lilium candidum has a perfect lily scent – exotic, but
not sickly. When you cultivate one, magical things happen:
you will be safe from malice and have the blessings of
the Virgin Mary, or goddess Isis, for this flower has been
associated with the most venerated of divine women.
Grow it with love and respect.*

♥ Do this in early summer. Find a beautiful, deep, pale-
coloured pot, and fill it with alkaline soil. Push some small
crystals, or semi-precious stones, into the earth and then
plant in it a lily bulb. Spirits of beauty and wisdom dwell
in the stones, and they will lend their graces and strength
to the blooms. As you plant, say: *'Precious spirits of these
stones, shine from the earth's heart and bones. May your
essence bless these flowers, let the lily wear your powers.'*
With the first scented flower, many blessings will come.

the *Lily* pharmacy

*Robert Frost said, in his poem 'Riders', 'We have ideas yet
which we haven't tried.' Lilies have such an exotic (and
slightly unsettling) scent that they entice us to consider
realms of untried emotions and passions, freeing us from
spiritual or sensual inhibitions.*

three magical recipes

♥ Try this recipe to create a **massage oil** that will open
up new frontiers with a lover or, indeed, treat skin rashes
such as eczema, with some kindness and to good effect.
Take the petals of three lily flowers and tear them, to
release their scent. Then, for seven days, infuse 50 ml
(2 fl oz) sweet almond oil with the petals. Agitate daily.
When the week is over, strain the oil and enjoy.

♥ You can also make a distillation of **lily-flower water**,
which has a history of use as a wonderfully powerful
cosmetic. Put into a saucepan the petals of 5 Madonna
lilies and 500 ml (17 fl oz) filtered water. Slowly bring to

the boil and then gently simmer for 30 minutes. Allow the flower water to cool, and use as a toner. Keep it in a bottle with the lid tightly screwed on, and put in a cool place. Try to use it up within three weeks.

♥ This **face mask** was once credited with easing lines away, as well as purifying and moisturizing the skin. Finely chop the petals of 3 Madonna lilies that are just beginning to open, and add to 2 tablespoons organic honey. Mix well. Pat the mask onto the face, avoiding your eyes. Leave on for 5–10 minutes, then rinse off with warm water. In some cases, this may reduce inflammation and soothe irritations, but in all events it should leave the skin soft, toned and enchanted!

Marigold — protection and healing

The pot marigold (*Calendula officianalis*) is one of the most attested and true for use in love potions, coming just behind roses and violets as the most efficacious flower for lovers; however, its scent is not to everyone's taste. It is a powerful healer, and protects one who wears it from falsehoods; in a posy or flower arrangement it gives the powers of persuasion to the woman! As a love charm, depend on the flower to avert jealousy; and rubbing the petals will prevent your suitor being dishonest, and rescue a maiden from the pain of unhappy love. Coming to fullest glory in early autumn, the marigold is, nevertheless, called the Summer Bride, as it opens its petals at first light, and closes them at sundown. If the flower is 'not open early in the day, expect a storm is on its way'!

Marigold kitchen witchery

Pot marigold to gardeners, calendula *to herbalists, this flower is the 'poor man's saffron' in the scullery. Steep petals in red wine, or put them in salads for colour and tang. Chopped petals will colour and flavour rice and add interest to omelettes. But best of all is pot-marigold bread:*

gather together

450 g (1 lb) self-raising flour; 60 g (2 oz) butter; 1 cup marigold petals; 250 ml (8 fl oz) milk; a pinch of salt

♥ Use organic flowers. Sift the flour into a mixing bowl, and work in the butter to resemble breadcrumbs. Toss in the marigold petals. Make a well in the centre, add the milk and salt, and mix with a knife to make a rough dough. Knead lightly on a floured surface, put into a round cake tin and cut a cross in the top. Bake for 30 minutes in an oven preheated to 180°C/350°F/Gas Mark 4. When you break open the bread, dedicate it to 'Our Lady'. Serve with butter.

magical Mary-gold blooms

The following spells bring magic into your house with pot-marigold flowers. Belonging to the Sun and precious to the Lady, the bloom offers double guardianship – it has a male and a female deity – and has been connected with prophetic dreams and protection.

♥ Celebrate a birth by making garlands of calendula flowers (pot marigolds) just as you would make a daisy-chain. Loop them over doors or cradles for luck on a christening, or naming, day. Placing petals under the pillow averts bad dreams; putting a few under the bed with some grains of sugar invites the angel of good sleep to get your child through the night without nightmares.
♥ Fill a muslin or cotton pouch with marigold petals, and take this with you for luck when facing an exam or the outcome of a legal issue. If you have a contract to sign, put a marigold in your lapel to avoid being taken advantage of.

♥ Fill a bag of muslin or linen with marigold petals and leaves, and tie under the bath taps. Run a bath for a triple effect: the soothing of skin irritations, especially sunburn; intensifying the lightness of fair hair; winning admiration from a lover or suitor after bathing. Three good reasons to try it!

♥ When a woman walks on marigold petals with her bare feet, it allows her to hear the fairies' laughter and singing, and gain welcome enchantment over a man.

♥ In the southwest of England (where I live) the flowers are called 'The Drunkards'; they are said to turn people into alcoholics if they look at the flowers for a long time. Actually, they are intoxicating steeped in warm red wine, making an interesting love potion that increases the sensation of joy!

Pansy many thoughts

Close cousin of the sweet violet, this is possibly the most potent single-flower love charm of all time. This little plant, called *Viola tricolor*, has half a dozen common names attesting to its efficacy in love matters: kiss her in the buttery, love lies bleeding, heartsease, cuddle me, and others. Pick the harlequin-faced flowers in cool weather, or when it rains, to ensure the best luck from every flower. Press a pansy in a pretty volume of verse for a friend or a lover who must travel away: you will stay forever on their mind! These flowers have a spirit all of their own; they will last longest, blooming or in a posy, for someone *they* admire, and if a pansy remains in a small vase for many days without fading, you are fortune's favourite.

bain des fleurs: a wild-Pansy bath for lovers

This flower has a reputation for its medicinal potency as a
tonic for the heart, and it has always been associated with
restoring heart distresses. This potion is a reinterpretation
of an ancient recipe that was given to young lovers for
their 'honeyed month' (honeymoon); it also has the most
delightful effect on the appearance of the skin.

gather together

1 cup pansy flowers and leaves; 500 ml (17 fl oz) cold
water; 1 tablespoon milk

♥ Use the herb pansy, *Viola tricolor* (use dried flowers if
fresh are unavailable). Soak the pansies in the water for an
hour. Then, boil for 30 seconds, turn off the heat and allow
the concoction to infuse for 20 minutes. Add to your bath
with the milk – it will help to soothe and brighten your skin,
gently increase libido, and rescue you from aches. For two,
add a few fresh pansy flowers to the water, and candlelight!

pense de moi: Pansies for a love cake

The idea of using flowers and messages in food is ancient; this is a romantic way to tell someone your feelings.

gather together

1 small, light sponge cake; 1 egg white; a little water; a few pansy flowers, trimmed of stems; caster sugar, for coating

♥ Bake a small, light sponge cake (or buy one from a good bakery). In a bowl, whip the egg white with the water until it is light and frothy. Holding each pansy flower carefully, paint the egg white onto the edges of the blooms, front and back, and then sprinkle with caster sugar, over a plate until the edges are gently coated. Leave to dry for 8 hours and then place the flowers into a heart shape on the top of the cake. Serve this at a romantic tea hour, or give as a gift to someone you love: the tiny blooms will win the shyest heart on your behalf!

Pansy *and rose wreath*: love for all

In the darkening days of autumn, pansies and roses are a late sign of colour in the garden. November is a magical month with many traditional feast days occurring, so make this wreath to attract good fortune and delighted smiles from guests in equal measure.

♥ Use a circular base woven from willow or rosemary stems, for added magical properties, and secure it with florists' wire. Onto the base, overlap equal-sized branches of bay or rosemary and bind them with wire until the base is covered. Tuck in, and pin if necessary, several blooms of pansies and roses, working with complementary colours (purple pansies and white or pink roses, perhaps). As you weave, sing to attract the fairies. Finish by trimming with ribbons that tone with the colour scheme, and hang the wreath on your front door to bring cheer and luck to your dwelling.

Carnation   sacred love and good fortune

Undoubtedly the prize token of love in Italy, the clove carnation (or pink, as it's known in England) is Jove's flower, and brings blessings and favour from the gods. It was used in the corona (crown) of ancient Greece and was thought to be the 'incarnation' of God in a flower. Cultivated in Tudor England for medicinal reasons, its delicious clove taste was also used to enliven ales, wines, sweets and sauces. It is the best single ingredient for a winter love potion, helping to intoxicate a lover with thoughts of you alone! When given as a gift, carnations betoken genuine affection, sending the message, 'I must see you soon.' In beauty rituals they help you look different and exotic; in a lapel they can be worn for impact and allure. Popular at weddings, carnations bring not only luck for love itself, but blessings for the life lived. Try to get proper clove carnations, as their fragrance is truer than that of commercial blooms.

hair *Carnations* to tell your fortune

♥ In the days before midwinter and Christmas (midsummer in Australia!), wear three carnations in your hair and dedicate them to the lady Cybele, Mother Earth (the sibyls were her priestess-oracles, great prophets of the Greco-Roman world, and carnations were sacred to them). Ask about the year ahead: if the top-placed flower wilts first, only the last years of your life will be difficult, and the year ahead will be calm; if the middle flower wilts before the others, only the first few months of the coming year will be demanding, and thereafter, luck and love will blossom. If the bottom-placed flower is the first to wither, the year ahead will be testing and full of hard work, and thereafter a love will come into your life bringing peace and serenity.

♥ Three white or pale-pink clove carnations in a bride's hair ensure health, wealth and happiness.

sops in wine: a winter love potion

This brew is delicious in winter potions, and Christmassy too! Make some for all your guests, or to offer someone you fancy …

gather together

1 teaspoon cinnamon; 1 teaspoon powdered ginger; ½ teaspoon cloves; 175 g (6 oz) brown sugar; 50 g (2 oz) roasted hazelnuts; petals from 6 clove carnations; 2 litres (3½ pints) red wine; some extra carnation petals to garnish

♥ Place the cinnamon, ginger, cloves, sugar, hazelnuts and petals in a large saucepan with the red wine. Heat very slowly, stirring regularly; take care not to let it boil. Transfer to a jug. Pour the potion into warmed tea glasses and pop the extra petals on the top. Given to someone special, success in love is certain; brides might be given this brew as an aphrodisiac. Try it at a yuletide feast to put all your friends in a merry (and lusty!) mood.

a lift for winter palates

Revisit olde England with this clove-carnation and lavender sorbet, perfect for a festive palate-cleanser or pudding.

gather together

350 ml (12 fl oz) water; 225 g (8 oz) white sugar;
2 tablespoons fresh or dried lavender flowers; ½ cup
fragrant clove-carnation petals (remove the 'heels');
1 tablespoon lemon juice; 1 teaspoon glycerine

♥ Put 250 ml (8 fl oz) water and half the sugar into a saucepan. Bring slowly to the boil, stirring, and simmer for a few minutes. Remove from the heat and allow the syrup to cool completely. Blend the lavender and remaining sugar, and add to the syrup; mix well. Leave to stand for an hour, then strain. Boil the remaining water, then remove from heat and stir in the petals. Brew for 20 minutes, strain and combine with the syrup. Add the lemon juice and glycerine; churn in an ice-cream maker for 15 minutes, and freeze.

further reading

BREMNESS, LESLEY, *Crabtree and Evelyn Fragrant Herbal: Enhancing Your Life with Aromatic Herbs and Essential Oils*, Quadrille Publishing, London, 1998. Astonishing and lavish resource book on herbs, flowers and scents, by a really well-informed author; an outstanding reference book.

BROWN, KATHY, *The Edible Flower Garden: From Garden to Kitchen – Choosing, Growing and Cooking with Edible Flowers*, Lorenz Books, London, 1999.

CREASY, ROSALIND, *The Edible Flower Garden*, Periplus Editions Ltd, North Clarendon, VT, 2000.

PHILLIPS, ROGER AND NICKY FOY, *Herbs*, Pan, London, 1990. Another first-rate reference book for vital information on herbs and flowers; one of my favourites.

resources

Try the following companies for more unusual requirements.

Candles and Supplies
500 Commerce Drive
Quakertown
PA 18951
USA
Tel: 215 538 8552
www.candlesandsupplies.com
Offers international mail order. Have soaps, lotions, creams and candles in an extensive range of fragrances, including hyacinth and carnation.

David Austin Roses Ltd
Bowling Green Lane
Albrighton
Wolverhampton
WV7 3HB
UK
Tel: 01902 376334
www.davidaustinroses.com
Supplies the most fragrant and beautiful roses I know of – perfect for all recipes.

Findhorn Flower Essences
Cullerne House
Findhorn
Moray
Scotland
IV36 3YY
Tel: 01309 690129
www.findhornessences.com
Wonderful essences made from local wildflowers and pure water from sacred healing wells. Offer international mail order.

obal Herbal Supplies
el: 1800 646 921 (Australia)
0800 0280 956 (UK)
1-877 553 4488 (USA)
ww.globalherbalsupplies.com
*ffers an international mail-
order service. Suppliers of a
st array of herbs, including
ganic violet leaf.*

elways Ltd
ngport
merset
A10 9EZ
K
el: 01458 250521
ww.kelways.co.uk
ail-order peonies of excellence!
elsea Flower Show medallists,
04.*

Neal's Yard Remedies
Head Office:
8–10 Ingate Place
Battersea
London
SW8 3NS
UK
Tel: 0845 262 3145
www.nealsyardremedies.com
*Offers an international mail-
order service. Superb herbs,
tinctures and potions, including
'Make Your Own' ingredients
for soaps and cosmetics.*

Soap Crafters Company
2944 S. West Temple
Salt Lake City
Utah 84115
USA
Tel: 801 484 5121
www.soapcrafters.com
*Everything you need for making
your own soaps and toiletries.
Mail order.*

The Soap Tub
The Mill House
Black Rock Mills
Waingate
Huddersfield
HD7 5NS
UK
Tel: 01484 340658
www.meltandpoursupplies.com
*Very good stockist of soap-
and cosmetic-making basics,
including peony petals and
hyacinth scent. International
mail-order service available.*

If you're in Australia, try
www.nurseriesonline.com.au
to locate individual nurseries
that supply specialist plants,
including peonies and sweet
violets.

63

about the author

Titania Hardie is Britain's most famous White Witch. She has a degree in psychology and has trained in parapsychology and horary astrology. She also has degrees in English literature and Romantic Studies. She has made hundreds of television appearances around the world, and has received widespread national newspaper and magazine coverage. Her previous titles include *Hocus Pocus*, *Dreamtime*, *Aroma Magic* and *Titania's Crystal Ball*. In 2002, Boots the Chemist (UK) successfully launched *Titania Hardie Beauty Spells*, an exclusive collection of magic and bath and beauty products.

acknowledgements

I am extremely grateful to Mary Walters for her original input – I owe her a fine cup of tea! Also Nick, Ian, Katie, Tessa and Elaine at Eddison Sadd, thank you for the opportunity to write about something I really love! To my darling husband Gavrik Losey, who not only tended our wondrous rose and peony garden, but checked the accuracy of so much of this information, heartfelt thanks: watch this space on Valentine's Day! And to the British Library I owe a debt of thanks for their time! Last, but never least, to Robert Kirby at PFD: grazie, Roberto!

EDDISON•SADD EDITIONS

Editorial Director *Ian Jackson*	Art Director *Elaine Partington*
Managing Editor *Tessa Monina*	Art Editor *Pritty Ramjee*
Editor *Katie Golsby*	Production *Sarah Rooney and*
Proofreader *Nikky Twyman*	*Nick Eddison*